MW01281878

# SCARS

## NEVER HEAL

JOANIE DUNCAN

 FriesenPress

One Printers Way
Altona, MB R0G 0B0
Canada

www.friesenpress.com

**Copyright © 2023 by Joanie Duncan**
First Edition — 2023

All rights reserved.

No part of this publication may be reproduced in any form, or by any means, electronic or mechanical, including photocopying, recording, or any information browsing, storage, or retrieval system, without permission in writing from FriesenPress.

ISBN
978-1-03-917851-9 (Hardcover)
978-1-03-917850-2 (Paperback)
978-1-03-917852-6 (eBook)

*1. BIOGRAPHY & AUTOBIOGRAPHY, PERSONAL MEMOIRS*

Distributed to the trade by The Ingram Book Company

**M**y name is Joanie Duncan and I'm going to tell you a story about myself. I'm going to tell you how that story affected my love life, my mom life and how it affects me emotionally and physically today. This story is a bit twisty in some parts, so I ask you to please pay close attention. It all has to do with when, where and how I became who I am today.

Back in 2009, I was in eighth grade at Richfield Springs Central School. Our teacher in study hall class, Mrs. Mellow, she handed us students these program brochures for BOCES. BOCES is Boards of Cooperative Educational Services. It's classes you take to learn about different services, in case you maybe want to work in that service in the future. So, I signed up for three different programs for BOCES. I'd do a half-day at my home school, Richfield Springs, and a half-day at Herkimer BOCES. The first program I signed up for was service and trade. I didn't start the program until the following year of 2010. In 2011, my second year of BOCES, I started trade industry. In that class I did a bit of mechanic work, some welding, building stuff and a tiny bit of planting. In 2012–2013, I graduated in culinary.

My first year of BOCES is how I met my friends and my ex-boyfriend, Jack. Jack and I were in the same class. Jack was about six feet tall and tan, with dark hair and brown eyes. I liked that Jack was always himself and that he thought of others before himself. He was always so caring and so sweet. He treated me really good. He was one of a kind, nothing like my past relationships.

Second year of BOCES, I was in trade industry. Jack was in construction.

Like any other class, everyone had to introduce themselves and what school district they came from. I was the only girl in the class. Jack's best friend Buddy, who I got close to over time and got to know well, was in the same class as me. Buddy watched over me a lot. I think it was because of Jack. My close friend Derek from the previous year of BOCES was in the same class as well. Derek's cousin Mel was also in the class. He was a good friend of Jack's. There were a few others, including my best friend Austin, who was not only in the same class as me in BOCES, but was also attending Richfield. Finally, our teachers were Mr. K and Mr. E.

By the time the first month of BOCES had gone by, everyone had gotten to know one another a little more. Almost every day before class, some of us from trade industry would wait outside in a group until the bell rang. There was Buddy, Mel, Noah, Austin and Jack and I.

Jack and I would say our goodbyes right there and then when the bell rang because we never got to see each other after class. His bus always arrived early at the end of the day to pick him up and take him back to his home school. The Richfield bus always came a few minutes after Jack's bus left. So, I only got to see him before class started, and I think that's why we drifted apart that year. We weren't seeing much of each other like we had over the summer.

I sort of got along well with the others in trade industry class. Everyone besides Noah. Noah was a cocky, mouthy, sarcastic kid who would always say smart remarks toward me and my best friend Austin.

Noah would always pick on Austin about his weight and give Austin and me dirty looks. Noah was especially mouthy to the teachers. Noah tried to fit in with Ken and Stefan because they were the smart-ass cool kids in the class. They liked trouble and didn't care much about anything. So, Noah tried to be like them. I did my best to ignore them all.

Noah wasn't well-liked in class. Everyone just tolerated him. Noah did his best to fit in, but I think Noah knew well enough that it wasn't working out well for him. I think that's what made Noah start talking to me to begin with: there was no one else, and he knew that I was a nice person. But based on the way he treated people, he didn't deserve to talk to anyone, including me.

Noah started talking to me when we got stuck being partners together. My thoughts when he started talking to me were, *What the fuck are you doing?* I thought to myself, *so you're going to be nice to me now. Start a conversation with me thinking I'll forget all the sarcastic remarks you've made toward me and my best friend?* Being the nice girl that I was, I talked back to Noah (not that I really had a choice—we were partners in class). But I also felt bad about how everyone else was treating him, though he did deserve it. I felt bad in a moment when I shouldn't have. But I did. Surprisingly, Noah was nice. We became friends after our first conversation together. Noah and I began to hang out more in class. I became a friend that Noah could talk to for relationship advice. I got to meet and know his girlfriend Stacy over time. She was a grade ahead of Noah and me, and she was in culinary class. It got to the point where Noah would talk to me about the good and bad things between him and Stacy almost every day.

I started to notice it was getting to be worse than good about Stacy. I usually kept to myself, but I told Noah that he should just tell Stacy whatever it was that was bugging him and just be honest about how he felt. Noah said that he already had plenty of times and that he would continue to do so. But instead of talking with her, one day out of nowhere, Noah walked up to me with Stacy and asked me to tell Stacy how he felt about her. I was not expecting any of it. Noah must have thought that I would really know how he felt from all the times we talked about Stacy in class. Noah wanted me to tell her because— apparently—Stacy didn't believe him.

I thought to myself, *you've got to be kidding me, right?* I stood there, up against a brick wall, all sorts of confused. I didn't know what to say. I was put on the spot, and it felt uncomfortable and awkward. I did know that the last time Noah and I had spoken about Stacy, he had wanted to break it off with her. But that wasn't my place to say. Right there in that moment, they both looked happy. I thought that maybe he had changed

his mind about breaking it off with her. That's how it looked to me, anyways. So, I told Stacy all the good stuff Noah had told me about her and how much he loves her and thinks about her all the time. I told her that Noah wanted things to work out between them. I went with that because I was put on the spot, and it wasn't my place to break it off for Noah. Noah just looked at me in serious, angry silence. I was confused about why he would be giving me such a hateful look. Without another word, Noah said, "Let's go," and he and Stacy left me standing there in silence as they walked Stacy to her class.

Noah was always late coming to class because of walking Stacy to hers. So, when Noah came walking into class, he'd always have to argue with the teachers about being late. After arguing this day, he sat down next to me and said, "Why did you tell Stacy that? I wanted you to help me tell her I don't want to be with her anymore."

I replied, "Well I thought that's what you wanted me to say. I'm sorry, I had no idea," Though I secretly did, but it wasn't my place to get involved.

I said to Noah, "You and Stacy looked like you worked it out. I didn't know what to say. I don't want to be the one to hurt her. That's on you."

Noah told me eventually why he wanted to break it off with Stacy: his feelings were growing for me. Noah knew I was in a relationship with Jack and that I was friends with Stacy. He knew it would start a war if I were to tell Stacy that he was interested in me. But I wouldn't do that. I knew that if I did, Stacy would get the wrong idea and think I wanted Noah.

So, from that point on, I tried to pull away from Noah a bit. I didn't want to listen to his complaining about Stacy anymore. I knew he was only doing it because of his feelings for me.

I didn't want any trouble, and I didn't want the fact that Noah was endlessly asking me out to hurt my relationship with Jack. After turning Noah down a handful of times, I got sick of it and told him that I wasn't leaving Jack and that if he didn't want to be with Stacy anymore then he should just leave. Noah's excuse was that he was afraid of Stacy, that she would flip out when he tried to end things and tell him he wasn't allowed to leave her.

I never believed that story. I told Noah that Stacy didn't control him. I gave up after telling him over and over to just leave her. Noah wasn't going to do anything about it anyways, so there was no point in trying to help him anymore. I certainly wasn't going to get in the middle of their relationship. I could tell Noah was trying to get Stacy and myself mad at each other.

For a good while, Noah quit asking me out and decided to work it out with Stacy. To be honest, I don't think Stacy really knew anything about the feelings Noah had been having toward her. I think he made it out to me that they were having issues when they really weren't.

There came a day when Noah was acting funny toward me, and I couldn't figure out why. I decided not to bug him and just left him alone. I thought that maybe he was just having a bad day. Next thing I knew, he'd come up to me in class and told me that there was something he wanted to talk to me about. I just knew something was off about him that day. I asked him what he wanted to talk to me about. He said he wasn't supposed to say anything, but then he blurted out that Jack, Stacy and Stacy's sister Ava had hung out days ago at Jack's place in Herkimer. Noah told me that the three of them had had a threesome. Noah said he had even heard the story out of Jack's mouth a few days ago.

What got me was that Noah hadn't spoken up about this sooner, especially after hearing it straight from Jack, and considering that Stacy is his girlfriend. I didn't bother to ask him about this though, because I thought that maybe Noah hadn't said anything because he was afraid that Jack might hurt him.

Either way, I was surprised to hear the story. I didn't think Jack was like that. I thought this might be something Noah had just made up to get stuff started so he could be with me. I was pissed off at this point. I didn't know what to believe. In my eyes, Noah was now a liar, Jack was a cheater and Stacy was a backstabbing friend. I thought to myself, *If Jack is spreading the story around, then how come no one else in the group told me?* This upset me because the group were my friends just as well as they were Jack's. In that moment, I felt like I had no one I could trust. But before I let my emotions get to me, I had to find out the truth for myself. I knew Noah liked me, but he also liked starting trouble. I wanted to confront Jack about it right there and then, but I wasn't going to be able to until the next day.

When The next day of BOCES, before class had started, Jack noticed that I was upset. He was always good at telling. He finally asked me what was wrong when I went and stood next to Noah instead of him. I confronted him about the threesome he supposedly had with Stacy and Ava in front of everyone in the group. Everyone went quiet. Jack smirked, looked over at Buddy and then looked back at me before saying, "I was walking, and I ran into a couple of friends."

I replied, "Yeah, which was Stacy and her sister."

Jack claimed nothing had happened, but I believe it was no coincidence that they ran into each other. I believe they set up to meet. Jack asked who I had heard it from, so I told him that Noah told me. Jack turned to Noah and said, "You need to shut your mouth and mind your business, or else I'm going to beat your ass. Worry about your own relationship."

Noah just stood there and didn't say anything. At this point, I still didn't know what or who to believe.

At the end of the same day, I was heading to the lobby doors to leave when I caught sight of Jack through them. It surprised me because he always left before I did. I wondered why he was still here. Maybe his bus was late. But the next thing I saw as I stood watching from the lobby doors was Stacy and her sister Ava approaching Jack. I saw the three of them exchange numbers and Stacy give Jack a hug and a kiss on the cheek. I was shocked, sad, confused and really starting to believe that what Noah had told me was true.

The next day, I told Noah what I had seen.

"See, I told you, but you didn't want to believe me," he said.

"I didn't know what to believe. Well, now I do," I replied.

I don't know why but after all this, I still stayed with Jack and Noah still stayed with Stacy. Jack and I managed to stick it out a couple more months, right up until he and Buddy started having issues with each other over something Jack had said about Buddy behind his back. The two were no longer on talking terms. Buddy said to me that Jack wasn't being himself lately and that he was acting different. Jack was turning into someone none of us recognized.

Buddy decided to get even with Jack. One day during class, he told me that Noah had told the truth about the threesome Jack had had with Stacy and her sister Ava. Buddy said that Jack was planning to break it off with me so he could go back to his ex, Delilah. They'd been on and off for years and they were now talking again. I just stood there looking at Buddy like I had just seen a ghost. I was shocked and speechless, my heart felt like it had dropped to my knees. It was the last thing I had wanted to hear. I didn't want to believe what I was hearing I had already been down and depressed with things back at home and this just added more to it.

Buddy said, "I hate to be the one to tell you this, but Jack's been lying. I just want to see you happy."

My mind took a second and went back through the memories I had of Jack and I together, like the time we danced to our song, "Island in the Sun" by Weezer and the times when we met each other's families. I snapped out of it, still standing there, thinking to myself, *it's all gone*. Why would he do any of this? Then, the doubt came into play. I started telling myself that I meant nothing to him. That everything was a lie, even the promise ring he put on my finger.

I told Buddy to tell Jack that I was done with him. Whether the two talked or not, at this point Jack knew that I now know the truth. And I never did say anything to Stacy about it. She still thinks I never knew and that she'd gotten away with being sneaky. I figured I'd let karma be a bitch. Whether I was karma or someone else was didn't matter. Either way, I knew it would come back to slap her hard in the face eventually. I just kept to myself.

I spent weeks getting over Jack. It didn't feel right without him. I felt lost and alone. But I knew it was for the best. Jack was always trying to make me jealous by being with other girls after the breakup. I sure did not care one bit because I knew what he was all about at that point.

A few weeks later, Jack told everyone in the group that he was moving away after winter break. So that was our last week with Jack. Everyone was beat up over it. I think Jack was the one who got the group together in the first place. Jack and Buddy finally made amends and Jack and I talked it out before he left. Buddy was especially torn up over Jack leaving. He felt alone and like he had no one to talk to. He even wanted to leave BOCES at one point, but I begged him to stay. He ended up staying because of me.

Throughout winter break, Jack was on my mind a lot. I secretly missed him. I hadn't wanted him to go. Part of me had been hoping that if he had stayed, there could have been a chance for us again. I was sad when he left, but I didn't want the others in the group to know.

# AFTER WINTER BREAK

When we all came back from winter break, our group was still together, and we all still stood outside in our spot. I was standing next to Mel, talking to him along with Stacy when suddenly, Mel pointed toward the buses and told us to look. Stacy and I looked over and saw Noah walking up from the buses to the lobby doors holding hands with Izzy, whom I knew from my previous year in service and trade. Mel and I looked over at Stacy for an explanation, but she was just as confused as the rest of us.

Eventually she said, "Well I guess he broke it off with me to go out with that chick,' but it won't be long 'til he comes crawling back and then he'll be boo-hooing to me about the mistake he made, like he always does." After that, she shrugged and said, "Oh well, not my problem anymore," before sending some dirty looks over at Noah and Izzy.

didn't group thought Noah and Izzy's relationship was funny. I think he was dating Izzy to piss Stacy off for some reason.

Stacy never explained why Noah left her for Izzy, and it doesn't make sense for Noah to leave Stacy just to piss her off. There was more to it, I believe. The way I see it, there are two sides to every story.

Noah was picked on badly over his relationship with Izzy because Izzy was chubby and had bright red hair. She was crazy and had piercings Not everyone cared for her, but I know I did. Izzy was nice and she and I had become good friends over the previous year. She wasn't part of the group, but she didn't care. She was unique and she always did her own thing.

Stacy was right though. It didn't take long for Noah to crawl back to her, apologizing for the mistake he made in going out with Izzy, just like she had said he would. I think Noah was just embarrassed being with Izzy because of her weight.

Later, I asked Izzy what had happened between her and Noah. Izzy said that she and Noah had only been together for a short while. No one even knew about their breakup until Noah was chasing Stacy again. Izzy said Noah seemed charming at first, but the sex was painful. Noah and Izzy had snuck around to do sexual things together because she wasn't allowed to have boys over at her residence. So, the two had hung out near the Herkimer high school. But the real issue was that Izzy was eighteen, and she was told by many close to her that Noah was only fifteen. Obviously, being older than him would get her into lots of trouble and Izzy was already on parole for drugs and drinking, so she asked Noah about his age. He told her that he was seventeen-and-a-half. Because Noah is the type to lie about things like this to get his way, Izzy went to the principal's office and asked Mrs. Phoenix to get ahold of Noah's mother to confirm his age. When it got back to Izzy that Noah really was only fifteen, Izzy confronted him. saying that she could have been nailed with rape and that she was already in enough trouble as it was. Her exact words were, "Nothing good came from him."

As Noah tried to get back together with Stacy, he lied to her by saying that nothing sexual ever happened between him and Izzy. But Stacy knew better and she 'told Noah that he wasn't touching her after touching Izzy. Izzy was also telling anyone that knew about her and Noah that he was lying and that he did have sexual intercourse with her.

Noah tried his darndest to make Izzy out to be the liar, but it was common sense—we all knew Noah was the one lying. He was so pissed off that Stacy didn't believe him and refused to get back together with him that he decided to make up a rumor about Izzy that she had aids When Izzy found out about the rumor, she decided to get even with him. She started telling people she was pregnant, even though she really wasn't. She told me she just wanted to piss Noah off some more and asked me not to say anything about her plan.

Izzy got Noah to believe her, right along with Stacy, who didn't want anything to do with him anymore. Noah believed the rumor so much he even admitted he got Izzy pregnant. He went days at BOCES thinking he got her pregnant, panicking the whole time. I watched him go through it all and I felt bad for him, so much so that I ended up telling him the truth—that Izzy wasn't pregnant. That started a huge argument in class between us because he was mad that I hadn't told him sooner. That I knew the truth the whole time. Noah and I didn't talk for a couple of days until we apologized to one another, though he had nothing to be sorry for. I was the one who knew the rumor wasn't true. A few days later, things between Izzy and Noah finally blew over.

After everything, Noah still wasn't giving up on trying to win Stacy back, and she did eventually end up giving him another chance. Things between them were alright there for a while, until Noah started complaining about Stacy seeing this guy in her culinary class. Stacy claimed 'he wasn't seeing anyone. I think Noah was finally feeling guilty about breaking it off with Stacy to begin with, because it got their relationship to the point where Stacy was at her wits end with everything. 'He finally saw what he had put Stacy through. From that point on' I didn't know what went on with Noah and Stacy didn't but the group noticed that Stacy wasn't hanging out with us as much. Whenever she arrived at BOCES, she would go straight to her class.

Time went on without any problems and issues for a while. The second half of the year was going by smoothly, and we now had about a week left of BOCES. Mr. K and Mr. E let us students have free time for the rest of that last week because there wasn't enough time left to start working on anything else. So, they either put on a movie for us to watch or we just sat there and talked or went on our phones until it was time for us to go home.

I was leaning up against the worktable, watching the movie that was on that day while the others were joking and messing around on their phones. I noticed Noah walking over toward me. He stopped right in front of me and said, "You're going out to eat with me a' a friend, I'm not taking no for an answer. Then you can decide if you want to go out with me or not for the last time."

I looked up at Noah and said, "You don't give up do you? What about Stacy?"

The two were on and off, so I had to ask. Noah claimed he had broken it off with Stacy. I didn't even know the two had gotten back together after the whole mess with Izzy. I wanted to ask Stacy myself if it was alright for me to go out with Noah. I figured it was the right thing to do, knowing that Stacy and I were friends, although I still had that whole memory of her and Jack in the back of my mind. But two wrongs don't make a right. Noah told me that I didn't have to ask Stacy and that I should trust him when he said that Stacy would be alright with it because Stacy was mad at him and didn't care what he did. I knew there was something odd about him not wanting me to say anything to Stacy, but I just jumped the gun and agreed not to anyway. I did however tell Noah that I had to ask my parents if it would be alright for me to go out with him first. Noah thought that was my way of getting out of it.

When I got home after BOCES that day, I did ask my parents if it would be ok to go out on a date with "this kid Noah from class." My parents were ok with it. My mother wanted to see a picture of him, so I went on his Facebook profile and showed her what he looked like. My mom said, "Well there you go, good-looking kid."

I messaged Noah on Facebook and told him my parents were ok with us going on a date.

I asked my brother-in-law, Scooter, if he could give me a ride down to Noah's place that weekend as I didn't have my driver's license yet and my parents were busy. Scooter agreed to give me a ride down to Mohawk, where Noah lived, and back.

When I got to Noah's place that weekend, a little boy answered the door. I asked if Noah was around. The little boy—his name was Brett who was Noah's youngest brother. I later learned he was Noah's half-brother— Brett yelled to Noah, and Noah came walking into the living room. I said hi to Noah as I walked into the apartment. It had a medium-sized living room, a small bathroom and stairs that led to a nice and big kitchen. The place felt cozy.

Noah's mother, Karen, was on the couch reading a book. She had a not-so-happy look on her face when she saw there was a girl in the apartment. She looked at me with a dead stare long enough that it made me feel uncomfortable. She then got up from the couch and walked out into the kitchen. Noah had an I-don't-care look on his face. I sort of knew at that point that Noah hadn't told his mother that I was coming over. I also got the vibe that Noah and his mother's relationship was bad. So, I just stood by the door to the living room, confused. Noah told me not to worry.

Noah introduced me to his other brother, Josh, who was a little younger then Noah who was sitting in a reclining chair watching a movie. It was awkward, no one made a sound we just looked at each other for a couple seconds. Noah then grabbed his wallet and said, "Come on." We left his place and started walking from Mohawk to a restaurant in Herkimer called Ponderosa, which is no longer around today.

"I wish I had a ride, but my mother won't give us one. She's mad."

When we got to Ponderosa, we waited at our table for food for about forty-five minutes. I was so nervous; I didn't know what to talk about. Noah spoke up and said, "It took you forever to give me an answer."

I just smiled and looked out the window. Dates weren't my thing. I was more of a stay-home-and-chill-in-my-own-space kind of girl. But I figured I'd give it a try.

When we had finished our meal, the table was a mess. I was going to clean it up, but Noah said, "The waiter's got it, it's their job not ours." So, I left it alone.

On the walk back to Noah's place, Noah was rambling on and joking about 'his and that. I didn't really hear him because I was in my own thoughts, trying to decide if I should give him a chance or not. I was thinking that if I did give him a chance, I would have to face everyone in the group, and I was questioning whether they would laugh at us Noah and I relationship and I would even have to face Stacy. I was thinking about turning Noah down just because I didn't want trouble with Stacy, but I was also thinking about what she had done with Jack behind my back. Jack had been everything to me. I know two wrongs don't make a right, but honestly, I wanted revenge on Stacy. On top of that, Noah had tried so hard for Noah to get with me for so long, plus he was nice enough to take me out.

So, I told Noah yes. He turned to me and looked confused to as what I was saying yes to and then he caught on and knew I meant a relationship and said, "Really?" I smiled and said yes again. Noah then reached out and grabbed my hand. He had a smile on that I hadn't seen before.

As we were walking, Noah wanted to take me to meet his friend who'd been like part of his family his whole life. Her name was Trixie. We walked over to her work, and he introduced us to one another. She was like a sister to him. She called Noah's mom, "Mom." We chatted with her for a bit before heading back to Noah's apartment.

When Noah and I got back to his place, we had to watch his little brother Brett while Karen left to drop Josh off at either soccer or football practice. I forget which one. Noah and I were watching *Talladega Nights*, and Noah and I decided to lay down on the couch while Brett sat on the floor. Noah started to get a bit touchy, and then he crawled on top of me, even though his little brother was right there. I told Noah, "Not in front of your brother." Noah stopped and laid back down beside me. Not long after, Karen came back to take Brett to his dad's. Noah, Josh and Brett all had the same mom, but Brett and Josh had a different da' than Noah. Noah's real father left when Noah was still a baby. I would find out later on down the road because his father had left.

After Karen and Brett left, Noah wanted to go over to his friend Kyle's apartment. Kyle lived right across from the Dollar General in Mohawk, which is where Noah's mother worked at the time. When Noah and I got to Kyle's, he introduced himself and his other friend who was over, Miles. Miles worked at the dollar store as well, so he knew Noah's mother.

Kyle and Miles had been playing a video game when Noah and I got there. Noah and I sat on the couch, and Kyle turned his chair around from the TV to face us. Kyle said to Noah, "How's Stacy going to take this?"

I looked over at Noah, shocked, and said, "I thought you broke it off with her?" Noah said he did, then he looked down at the floor.

Kyle spoke up then and said, "Nah, I'm just playing man," and laughed. He then started talking about his relationship with a girl he'd been with for a while. After a bit, Kyle got up from his chair and walked out to the kitchen, calling Noah after him. This left just Miles and I in the living room. Miles waited until Noah was out in the kitchen with Kyle before spinning his chair around from the TV to face me and saying in a very low tone, "You have no idea what you're getting yourself into, do you?"

I asked Miles what he meant by that, and his response was that I would find out in the long run. I pleaded with Miles to explain, but Miles just kept saying, "You'll see."

Miles turned away from me to face the TV again. I was scared, nervous, upset and confused about why he had said that to me. I knew by his actions that there was more to be said and that Miles wanted to say it, and I wanted to know what it was, badly. But I knew it wasn't good. I did my best to shrug it off because part of me doubted Miles a little. I told myself that maybe he was one of those kinds of people who just says things to start something. But something also made me believe Miles. I never said anything to Noah, but I did always keep what happened in my mind. Turns out that I would eventually find out what Miles had meant.

As Noah and Kyle walked back into the living room, Noah asked me, "Are you ready to go?" We said our goodbyes and went back to Noah's place. Those words from Miles stuck with me the rest of the time I spent with Noah that day. It wasn't long after we got back that I had to go home.

Monday came back around, and I now had to face the group about being with Noah, which was a big part of what I was worrying about over the weekend. When Noah and I arrived at BOCES, the group looked at us with confusion and shock. They certainly weren't happy. They all started asking questions. They also thought our relationship was funny, which, of course they would, they'd thought the same about Noah and Izzy too. They picked and picked on us non-stop until Noah just wanted to go inside. Something about that was suspicious to me though. I didn't think he wanted to go inside just because they were picking on us. I thought there was something he wasn't owning up to, so he wanted to go and hide out. I was asking myself then if he really did break it off with Stacy. I had asked Noah if he had, and he'd said yes. But now I was about to find out for real.

Stacy was arriving. As she walked toward the group, Mel went to meet her, stopped her, took her to the side and told her everything about Noah and me. Noah and I watched from inside the lobby doors, and we could tell that Stacy was shocked and very angry. She came toward the doors, burst in, walked up to Noah and slapped him in front of everyone in the lobby, yelling, "How could you do this to me, you knew we were together!" She then turned to me. "And you, how could you do this? I thought I could trust you. I thought you were my friend, but I guess not." She then walked back out the doors and stood with the rest of the group. I followed her outside, trying to explain, Noah trailing behind me.

"I'm sorry, I had no idea. I had wanted to come to you about it because I wanted to be a real friend."

"Well, a real friend doesn't go behind their friend's back and sleep with their friend's boyfriend." Stacy smirked and then said to me, "You have no idea what a real friend is so get out of my face."

I tried again. "Noah said he broke it off with you and that you were ok with it, so I didn't come to you like I wanted to."

Stacy laughed. "And you believed him? No, I'm not ok with it and we were still together, so get away from me."

"No, we are going to solve this."

"You better get out of my face and away from me."

At this point, I turned to Noah. "Why did you lie to me? You said you broke it off with her." I was so frustrated and mad. I walked back inside and Noah followed me in, saying again and again that he was sorry.

Eventually, I forgave him. It was his first mistake, and I had remembered that he had once told me that he was afraid of

Stacy. But I made sure that he was done with her for good this time. I was upset that my friends had turned on me. They looked at me as a boyfriend stealer. I felt like I had no one to hear my part. All of my friends in the group, aside from Buddy (and Austin, but he had moved away by then), disliked me and were talking crap about me.

It even went outside of our group. This girl Ellie, she had always followed Stacy around like a lost puppy. Well, she had some secrets of her own. Weeks before Noah and I got together, she told me that she had been talking to Noah behind Stacy's back and that at one point, Noah was even going to leave Stacy for her. I'm pretty sure Ellie and Noah had even slept together.

Now, I barely knew Ellie. I had only ever talked to her a few times. But just because Ellie was shoved up Stacy's ass and the fact that Stacy now hated me had Ellie figuring she should get her nosey, tooth-faced self-involved in something that had nothing to do with her. She joined in and started talking crap about me and Noah. I think she was just a bit jealous because she was once involved with Noah too. Ellie continued to talk crap to the point that when I confronted her, she and I almost scrambled right there in the lobby.

"If you've got something to say, now is the time to say it, while I'm standing here."

"Why, what're you going to do?"

"I'll show you what I'm going to do."

"You aren't going to do nothing."

"You want to bet?"

"You wouldn't be saying any of this if Stacy were here."

I smirked at this. "Go get Stacy. I'll tell her the same damn thing."

Buddy was standing with me, telling me to calm down and just ignore Ellie and go to class. So, I started walking away, until Ellie said something under her breath. I turned right around walked up to Ellie's face again and said, "You want to do this? We can fucking do this right here, right now." I started taking off my jacket.

Buddy stepped in between us. "No, no, come on, she's not worth it, just calm down. Come on, let's go."

"This bitch has been running her mouth just because Noah and I are together and I'm getting sick of it all."

"Just, come on." Buddy got us to separate, and he and I started walking away to class, leaving Ellie standing there, watching us.

Ellie waited until I was a distance down the hall before yelling, "Yeah that's what I thought." I stopped to turn around, but Ellie had already stormed off.

Shortly after that, the BOCES principal, Mrs. Jenkins, pulled me out of class for questioning because Ellie had said that I had threatened her in the lobby. I explained to Mrs. Jenkins what had happened and what had been said.

"I'm going to have to suspend you if you don't stop, because we can't have that kind of behavior here."

I was so pissed off. I really wanted to tear Ellie's head off at that point, and I was just so done with my old friends from the group talking crap. "Stop? You're telling *me* to stop? She's the one whose been running her damn mouth."

"Calm down and watch your mouth."

"Well do your damn job or else I'll take matters into my own hands."

"Don't tell me how to do my job and stop with the attitude or you're going to be suspended."

"Whatever, do what you got to."

"What did you just say?"

"You heard me."

"Alright, you done it." Mrs. Jenkins started walking away then, so I walked back to my classroom.

I was suspended for the last couple days before BOCES ended for the summer, and it made no sense to me why. But that was the last time I ever saw Ellie. The group also knew that next year wouldn't be the same. Mel had gotten into a lot of trouble with the law. Buddy ended up moving away and Derek had decided to stay at his home school the following year. The group had broken up.

# SUMMER 2012

School was out, and Noah and I continued to see one another. I lived out in the country while Noah was still in the Mohawk Valley. One hot summer day, I went back to Noah's place again. This time, it was just Noah and I at his place. We watched a movie, and Noah showed me around his apartment this time, so I saw more than when I had just been standing in the door the first time, I was over.

Noah took me to the kitchen. I sat up on the countertop. Noah was standing in front of me, leaning toward me. Noah reached above my head into the cupboard, pulled out a bottle of Irish rum and told me to try it. I took a sip, and it burned my throat. Noah laughed at me before taking a sip himself and putting the bottle away.

We went for a walk to the dollar store where Noah's mother, Karen, was working. When Noah and I got there, Karen was outside on her break, talking with another employee. Miles was there too. He came walking over and I said hi before going quiet again while he and Noah and Karen and the other employee talked for a bit. Then Noah and I left to go back to his place.

When Noah and I got back to his place, Noah wanted to go upstairs. He showed me around the other rooms before we went into his bedroom. I walked in and stopped in the middle. My back was turned toward him while he stood in the doorway, talking to me. I stood there for a good few minutes, listening to him talk. He then came up from behind me and hugged me. I turned around to hug him back. He looked down at me and kissed me. My heart was racing. I was so nervous but so warm, like I was melting. He was so sweet and so good to me. It felt like for once I finally had someone who was all about me. Being betrayed by Jack had really hurt me, and now I was drawn to Noah because he had wanted me for so long, hadn't stopped until he had me and even now, he still wanted me.

Noah let go of me, walked over to his air mattress and sat down before calling me over to sit next to him. Noah noticed I was nervous. He started kissing me, and the next thing I knew, things were going further. He had crawled on top of me and had started undoing his pants. His hands wandered up under my skirt and pulled my panties off.

After it was all over, we got dressed and laid back down. I asked Noah if he could hold me. He did. Noah had known all the right things to say and ways of saying them to get me to sleep with him and forgive him whenever we fought.

After a while, we got up and went for another walk. This time he took me to see a woman who was like a second mom to him. She lived right around the corner from his apartment. I don't remember her name, but she was a sweet lady. We hung out there for a bit before going back to Noah's apartment. When we got back, we had run out of things to do, so we started playing truth or dare. I dared Noah to go out on the porch and dance. I didn't think he was going to do it, but he did, and he continued to do it while traffic went by. People driving by in their vehicles would look over at him with a disturbed look on their faces. I laughed so hard.

After dancing, we order some pizza, and it was getting late. After we ate, we were sitting on the couch, and I crawled on top of him to sit facing him on his lap. Slowly we ended up lying down on the couch together before he got on top of me. Then we both heard a beep and Noah sighed. We got up, I looked out the door window and I realized it was my ride. So, Noah walked me out.

My older brother Allen and my uncle Henry were there to pick me up. I introduced them to Noah, and my brother and Noah recognized each other from when my brother used to go to BOCES a couple years back. I guess Noah had witnessed a fight my brother had been in at BOCES. Allen and Noah talked for a bit and then I gave Noah a kiss and hug goodbye. On the way home, I blurted out that I missed him already. My uncle and brother laughed. Allen said, "Seems like a nice kid."

I just smiled because it felt good to be treated well. Noah had showed me that he wanted me all the time, that I meant a lot to him. It felt good to start fresh in a new relationship.

Noah would ride his bike from Mohawk to Richfield just to see me. I always said he was crazy for doing that. He would say each time, "Well, I want to see you."

Noah's mother wouldn't give him rides. Noah and his mother had a love-hate relationship. Whenever Noah wanted something is when he would try getting along with his mother. I asked Noah why he and his mother don't really get along and he said that it was because Karen chose her relationships over her own kids. That's why all of her kids had times when they didn't want much to do with her. Josh, the oldest, eventually stopped seeing her completely. I don't know why. But Brett and Noah continued to see her. Noah told me that there had been one guy in their lives who had put hands on him multiple times when he was younger. I don't know where Josh and Brett were while this was happening to Noah.

# FATHER'S DAY, JUNE 9, 2011

Karen wanted to rebuild her porch. She had a friend she knew from high school named Duke that she called up to help her. Noah met the guy and talked with him for a bit until Duke and Karen left to get more lumber. When they got back, they worked on the porch for a little bit, then took a break. Karen invited him in for a few beers before taking him to the bedroom to show him pictures and talk history for a while. Then he went back out to finish the porch. Noah had called me up to tell me all this over the phone.

"Some guy named Duke who helped my mom with the porch claims he knows you."

"Wait, what?"

Noah described the Duke that I knew: tall, tan, bandana, sunglasses and tattoos.

"Oh my god I do know him, that's my sister's boyfriend!" I shouted.

"Is it really?"

"Yes."

"Well, my mom and him went in the back room."

"Wait! Did they do things?"

"I don't know. Must have, because he came out smiling after."

I couldn't believe what I was hearing, but at the same time I could because of the way my older sister Lorraine would talk about Duke and how he would act around other females, trying to impress them by putting her down. My sister and Duke's relationship had been complicated for as long as I could remember. They had been together since I was five at this point in time I believe I was 17. they had two kids together. Around the same time that Duke helped Karen out with her porch, Karen was also seeing some married guy named Dennis who lived in the trailer park in Mohawk. Dennis was a bald and slightly chubby tattoo artist. Dennis loved having more than just one female to mess around with. I think Karen knew this, but he didn't care. He also hid these women from his wife. Duke and Dennis knew each other from way back, and they were still good friends.

A few weeks after Duke fixed Karen's porch, my sister Lorraine started hanging out with our cousin, Ann, that we had not seen in years. I believe Ann was the one who reached out to Lorraine or Duke, but I don't really remember. Ann started going over to my sister's just about every weekend. They had bonfires and cookouts, and of course they were drinking and getting high. Ann left her guy she was with at home with their kids most of the time. The guy's name was Shane, and I'm not sure if he ever went over to my sisters at all. I went a couple times. Sometimes my sister's kids would be there or they would be with their friends for the night. But mainly it was just Duke, my sister and Ann. Every weekend.

Things were going smoothly until one weekend, Ann and Lorraine had partied too much and gotten too drunk and too high. Duke, who had just gotten back from a friend's house, had also been drinking, and he stayed up long enough to have a bit more with Lorraine and Ann. Lorraine then suggested that they have a threesome. Ann agreed, but Lorraine warned her that it would just be for one night and that Ann wasn't allowed to develop feelings for Duke or see him on her own. Ann agreed and the threesome went ahead.

Things didn't go as Lorraine intended. Ann started coming to the house just about every day, hanging around Duke in a way that made Lorraine uncomfortable. She was certain Duke was cheating on her and eventually confronted Ann, who accused her of being a bad partner to Duke. Lorraine then went to Shane and told him everything about the threesome and her suspicions about Ann and Duke, and then they hooked up as well. Ann of course was furious when she found out. Ann ended up getting pregnant with Duke's child. Lorraine insisted that she get an abortion and had threatened Ann to do so. Ann did, but only after telling Shane that it was his. Duke found out and was disgusted with Lorraine for threatening Ann. His relationship with Lorraine got worse and worse, but they stayed together for the sake of their kids. A couple weeks went by, and things were getting calmer between Duke and Lorraine, now that Ann was no longer in contact and involved with them. But every once in a while, Lorraine would bring up Ann's name and they would still fight about it.

One summer day, Duke and Lorraine invited me, Noah, my mom and my dad up for a cookout. This was when my sister first met Noah. Duke recognized him from when he helped build Noah's mother's porch. My sister knew Duke had helped someone build a porch, but she didn't know who. The moment she met Noah took me back to our conversation about Duke and his mother in the back room. Of course, my sister had no idea about any of it. Noah and I also had no idea if Karen and Duke actually did things or not. We all had a good time at the cookout though.

My sister, Duke, Noah and I hung out a few times. But this one time, I remember my sister calling me up, saying Noah was at her place. I wanted to go there to see him, so Lorraine sent Duke to come gets me on his motorcycle. Duke dropped me off because he had somewhere else to go. When I walked in and saw Noah, he was sweating heavily. I asked him why he was sweating so much. He told me it was because he had left to go do something and then rushed back over. My sister then came walking out of her room and asked Noah if he was ok. That threw me off. My sister took me to her room and the bed was a mess. I started thinking that something had happened between Noah and my sister. I started feeling betrayed by both. I was very upset. I had a burning sensation running through my body as I asked myself, *would she really do that to me?* My sister wasn't in a good place with Duke and Noah was acting funny. I let it go only because I didn't want to believe it and I didn't have any evidence. I was only going by how they had acted. I didn't even know if my sister's bed had already been a mess or not. So, I let it go, we all waited until Duke got back and then we went to the fair.

There were a few times when Noah and I would visit my sister while Duke was at work. Lorraine would come get me, and Noah would ride his bike up Vickerman Hill to meet me at my sister's. Lorraine would always talk to Noah and me about how she was feeling after everything that had happened between her and Duke and Ann. Lorraine kept living in the past. She was badly damaged over it all. She cried many tears and wanted to give up plenty of times because of it. She felt that there was nothing to do to fix the pain. She got deeper into marijuana.

One of those days when Duke was at work, the three of us were sitting around Lorraine's kitchen table and Noah decided to tell her that he had met Duke already because it was his mother that Duke had helped build the porch for. Noah also told my sister that Karen and Duke had gone into their back room with the door shut. So, my sister thought Noah's mother and Duke had done things together. I just sat there at the table in silence, because I knew that once Duke got home, my sister was going to confront him about it. I didn't want trouble.

When Duke got home that day, Noah and I were still there, but we were outside. Duke walked in and my sister did exactly what I knew she was going to: she confronted Duke about what Noah had told her. She started accusing Duke, which made Duke storm outside to yell at Noah to leave.

A few weeks Duke and Lorraine came up to visit my mom and dad. During the visit, Lorraine had something she wanted to talk to me and mom about, so we went into mom and dad's bedroom. She told us that she had been sneaking around with some guy named Dennis from the trailer park. She said that Duke had introduced her to him because he was a tattoo artist and she had wanted a tattoo of a butterfly on her chest. She said that while she was getting her tattoo done, Dennis whispered sweet things to her and slipped his number to her when Duke wasn't looking. From that point on, she'd been sneaking messages over to Dennis and sneaking over to his trailer at night—he only lived right around the corner from her. She would lie to Duke about where she was going. After a while, Duke started wondering why she kept going out every night. She told us not to say anything about any of this.

One night, my sister went over to see Dennis. When she got there, she saw a familiar face. It was Noah sitting on the couch. She saw a woman with Noah, and, putting two and two together, figured out that the woman must be Noah's mom, who Duke had helped with the porch. Lorraine knew she was caught red-handed. Noah must have told his mother that Lorraine was my sister and that she was dating duke.

I believe this same night; Duke got a phone call from a friend who knew Lorraine was sneaking over to see Dennis. The friend told Duke what Lorraine was doing. Duke didn't seem surprised, but he sure wasn't happy. Duke had been wondering why Lorraine kept asking him if he needed anything from down in the valley late at night, almost every night. Lorraine was just looking for a reason to go around the corner to see Dennis.

This started even more problems between Duke and Lorraine when Duke confronted her. They fought about Dennis and my sister found out that Duke and Ann had met up once again. There was just no trust, nothing but arguing all the time. I believe my sister did all of this because she couldn't get over the Ann thing. It really damaged her. She wasn't herself for the longest time. She would do nothing but cry. It changed her. Seeing her like that made me feel bad for her. I wanted to help her, but there was nothing I could have done. Honestly, she had done the damage to herself. But we are all humans, and we all make mistakes.

Dennis eventually moved away and let one of his friends, Richard, take over the trailer. Karen was no longer seeing Dennis and neither was my sister. Noah said his mother had started seeing Richard. They were seeing each other for about a month when Karen moved into the trailer park with Richard and his daughter, who was about the same age as Noah. Noah wasn't happy about moving into the trailer park. He complained that Richard wasn't right for his mom, that he did drugs and drank a lot and that he was mouthy and very bossy. Noah didn't see why his mother wanted to be with him. Noah felt uncomfortable around him.

I went over to the trailer park one day to hang out with Noah for the day. Later, when Noah asked Richard if I could stay the night, Richard made a comment about us having sex, which creeped me out. Thankfully, I knew my dad wouldn't let me stay anyways, and sure enough when I called, he insisted that I walk to my sister's house around the corner and stay there for the night.

A couple weeks later, my sister threw another cookout, and she invited me, my mom and my dad. We got to my sister's place and hung out there for a little bit before I asked my father if I could walk over to Noah's place and stay there until they were done with the cookout. He was alright with it. So, I walked over to the trailer park. I didn't see a vehicle outside, but I knocked on the door anyways. No one came to the door. I waited a few minutes and then knocked again. It was then that I started hearing moans coming from Noah's bedroom, which was the one closest to the door. I knocked again and still got nothing. So, I left and started walking back to my sister's place. I was shaking and upset from what I had heard. I was thinking to myself, *Would Noah cheat on me?* When I got back to my sister's I told my parents that he wasn't answering, and I told them what I had heard. They recommended waiting a half hour and then trying again.

I waited that half hour, walked back over and knocked again. Noah answered this time. I asked him if he had heard me knocking earlier and I told him that I had heard moans. He said no one else was there and that he had been asleep. I walked in, we talked for a bit, then we started making out on the couch. I noticed he had no boxers on, so I asked him why. He said he didn't have any clean ones left. Now in the back of my mind, I'm thinking, *Alright, I was just here thirty minutes ago and heard moans, and now he doesn't have any boxers on. Would he really lie to me?* I shrugged it off and decided to watch a movie with him until my parents came to pick me up.

Close to the end of summer, Noah's mom and Richard moved out of the trailer park into a new place together. Noah ended up getting kicked out because of his mouth and attitude. I didn't know exactly what Noah had done to be kicked out, or exactly when it had happened. All I knew was that Noah stayed with a middle-aged couple, Kate and her husband Jacob, and their two kids, Mike and Ruby, in the trailer park for a while.

My sister snuck Noah over to her house whenever Duke wasn't home so I could see him on weekends. Noah always left around the time Duke was expected to be back so he wouldn't get caught there.

Around this time, my parents were looking for a new place to live, and eventually they found a place in Fly Creek. It was about a thirty- to forty-minute ride away from Noah. I was worried that I wasn't going to be able to see him as much.

The day my parents were moving their stuff to their new place, Noah and I were at my sister's, visiting. I wanted to stay longer, but my father wanted my help to move stuff, so my uncle, Henry, and my brother, Allen, came to pick me up.

Noah and my sister exchanged numbers, and I was ok with that. After I left, Noah still hung out at my sisters for a while. Noah went to my sister's three days in a row when Duke wasn't around. Noah went back home late those three nights. It started to worry Kate and Jacob; the people Noah was staying with in the trailer park. My sister sent Noah dirty jokes through messaging when he was at home.

One night, Kate went over to my sister's while Noah was there. she knew where my sister lived because Noah either showed her or told her. Kate knocked on my sister's door and when it opened, she let into my sister, yelling at her, "Noah has been coming home drunk every night," and throwing Noah's age in my sister's face. My sister let right back into Kate and kicked her out.

After this, my sister put a stop to Noah coming over. I think Kate may have told Noah's mother what Noah had been doing and who he'd been hanging out with. Noah had told his mother that Lorraine was messaging him dirty jokes, and I'm not sure if Noah's mother got ahold of Duke and let him know what was going on, but either way, a war started between Duke and Lorraine when Duke found out that Lorraine had been sneaking Noah over to the house when he wasn't home. My sister had technically been sneaking Noah over to see me, but she had continued to do this when I wasn't there. Duke didn't want Noah there at all. I have had a lot of emotions about the situation, and questions, like, why when I'm not there? I have had suspicions about them being there by themselves. I was not comfortable with it at all. But I didn't want to be the one to tell Noah what to do either.

I look back on all of it now. And the feelings I got today about the whole situation, knowing regardless of not getting the real truth, is that it is what it is and I don't really care about it anymore. If it happened, it happened. I don't care about it, but it does hurt a little. But the hurt that I do still have, isn't as hurtful as it was back then.

# FALL 2012

School was starting back up again, and I wondered if I was going to have to go through the same drama I had gone through the previous year. Noah and I were in culinary class together and so were Stacy, but she was a grade ahead of us so she was in the morning class and we were in the afternoon class. Sometimes BOCES would have special events, which meant the morning class and the afternoon class would have to work together to make food for these occasions. So, I knew Noah and I were bound to run into Stacy eventually.

It didn't happen until months into the year. We finally had a special event and everybody from the morning and afternoon classes all had to be in the kitchen to cook and clean. Noah and I saw Stacy as we were standing next to the dishwasher helping others. Stacy kept giving us dirty looks. I was standing there for a while and when I happened to turn around, I realized that Noah had gone over to stand next to Stacy. I couldn't figure out why he would be standing over there. But then I saw that he was trying to talk to Stacy, not caring that I was watching him do it. He had been distant from me for most of that day already, and now that I knew what he was up to, I was mad. He was trying to win her back, just like any other time he was with someone else. He always went back to Stacy.

After the event, most of the morning and afternoon classes went to check out the career fair. I was standing in the middle of the aisle with tables on both sides of me, about six steps apart from each other. Noah was standing in front of me when I noticed Stacy, who saw me look at her. She spoke up.

"Joanie, if you got something to say, say it to my face."

"In fact, I do." I walked up to Stacy and started trying to explain myself once again. "Stacy, I miss being your friend, and I'm sorry for everything. I really didn't know he was still with you. He told me he broke it off with you."

"I'm sorry you're such a skank," Stacy said, and she shoved me

"I'm sorry you're such a bitch," I said as I pushed her back.

She came at me then, headbutting me before putting me into a headlock. I took my elbow and started hitting her in the side until she let loose, then I put her into a headlock and started hitting her in the head. She elbowed me in the forehead, and I let go. We came crashing together again so that her hands were on my shoulders and mine were on hers. I used my fist to hit the middle of her arms to try and break free from them, but it wasn't working, so I used my fist to hit her on the side of the face instead. She bent over from the blow but then started trying to spear me from below as I hit the top of her head. She managed to pull me down and now that I was bent over, she was trying to grab my nose and snap it. She ended up giving me a bear hug, so I grabbed her hair in order to get her to let loose. She let go and then we were pulling each other's culinary coats before she grabbed my hair. I snapped back but was able to whack her arm away, pull her in with one hand, and swing and hit her in the face.

There were some marines at the career fair, and at this point, some of them grabbed her, but she pulled me with her. She hit me on the top of my head, and I saw stars. It took me a moment to snap out of it, but when I did, I dove underneath a marine's arm and grabbed Stacy's head and dragged my nails down her face. She scratched me back and hit me before the marine got a hold of me. I kicked her hand away one last time, and then we were separated.

I started walking away when Stacy yelled, "I'll kill you bitch." I stopped and turned around with my fist up, and she yelled again, "Bring it bitch." I kept walking as I flipped her off.

I had to go to detention. That's where I met this kid named Chase. He asked me what I was in there for, so I told him. He knew Stacy. Didn't talk highly of her. Said in so many words that she slept around. Thought she was just nasty.

A couple days later, Noah called me up saying he wanted to talk to me about something. But, instead of telling me what it was, he put Kate and Jacob's son Mike on the phone and had Mike break it off with me for him. Apparently, he was going to try and get back with Stacy, and not only that, but he had been crushing on a girl in our class for a while. I started crying and got off the phone. I felt, yet again, betrayed by someone who

I thought loved me. I cared so much for Noah. My heart was so broken, because I was that girl that he once wanted so badly and fought so hard for so long to get. Just to leave me broken. He had made me feel like for once I had someone who wanted to stay with me. And then he just left me.

During the days of detention at BOCES, I got to know Chase. He had the same amount of detention days as me. We exchanged numbers, began talking more and more and eventually started dating. He was nothing like Noah. I think I went out with Chase just to fill an empty spot that had been left by Noah. Not only that, but I wanted to make Noah jealous. I just wanted Noah to feel how he made me feel.

Noah found out about Chase and me. I think he stalked my Facebook page. He called me up on Thanksgiving and said," Wow, you're dating one of my friends on Thanksgiving." I laughed on the inside and replied, "Well you're the one who broke it off with me, so get over it."

From that point on, Noah would make smart remarks toward me. But it wasn't long until my relationship with Chase ended. My best friend added him on Facebook and started talking to him behind my back. Chase went along with it and they both decided to meet up and have sex behind my back too.

I found this out after he ended it with me. I just woke up one morning and saw that my best friend, Mitch, and Chase were in a relationship on Facebook. The only thing I got from him was that he fell for her and he's sorry it didn't work out with the two of us. So, I started harassing Mitch that night on Facebook because she stole my boyfriend and had sex with him behind my back. I knew she wanted him once I had shown a picture of him to her on the bus one day and she made the comment, "I'd fuck him," but I didn't think she would do that to me. But she did. Chase was just a fill-in, and I didn't really care about him or why he would cheat on me, but I did care about Mitch because she was my best friend. I didn't want to believe that Mitch would do that to me. She meant a lot to me and I loved her. She was my best friend. I was so fucking hurt over it.

I look back on it all today and even though I'm over it, I certainly trust no one.

The next morning, I was called into the principal's office at my home school. The principal wanted me to give her my email and password to Facebook so she could see the threats and harassment I posted to Mitch. So I did, Principal Pearl then said, "Well, I'm going to have to suspend you for two days."

I was shocked and mad. "What! You're going to suspend me, but Mitch won't get suspended?

"She didn't threaten you."

"Well make it three days then."

I got up from my chair and ran out the door. I heard Mrs. Pearl yell, "Stop her!"

I ran down to the gym, opened the doors and yelled, "Where is she?" One of the girls in the gym class pointed at Mitch, Mitch made to run but I stopped her, spun her around by her hair and hit her on top of the head. I pulled her near me, but the principal had caught up to me by then and gotten my hands off Mitch, so I swung and punched the principal in her nose instead. Mrs. Pearl spun me around and said, "Move!"

I turned back around and told her with my fist up, "Don't you fucking touch me, or you'll get it too."

"You already got your fair share," she replied.

I went back to look for Mitch. The students from the gym class had locked her in the coach's office with the lights off. I remember yelling, "I know you're in there, you fucking bitch." I was so mad; I destroyed the gym room while screaming "I want blood!" I also yelled about wanting to kill her. My parents were called to the school, I ended up arrested and I was transferred to Cooperstown hospital for flipping out. I remember my body felt heated and I had a bloody taste in my mouth from being so pissed. I blacked out. When I got to the hospital, a doctor come in to talk to me about going away for a month in some other kind of hospital. I told her no. So, they set me up with a counselor. I stayed in that hospital for two or three days.

When I returned to school from suspension, Mitch was told to stay away from me. But Mitch would walk by me and say she didn't care. I just smirked and shrugged it off. Noah and I worked out our problems.

and ended up together again. Even in the moment, I had thought to myself that I was falling back into the pattern I had gone to the hospital for. I was going back to someone who, in the beginning, I was sure wasn't going to leave me, but eventually would.

Mitch talked so much crap about me and Noah whenever she saw us because of course she and I hated each other at this point, and it was just another way for her to talk about me to others. But I didn't care anymore. I just continued with my days.

Eventually, Mitch and I apologized to one another. I don't really remember how we made amends, but I believe she was the one to apologize first. She was still with Chase. She apologized for what she did, and I just told her not to do it again. Mitch said, "Let's not have any guys come between us ever again," and I agreed. Mitch never liked Noah; she told me this during our conversation. But she supported me anyway.

Noah and I were doing well in our relationship—no fighting, staying solid. The love was better. Things were back to normal, the way it had been when we had first gotten together. A week or two after getting back together, I started noticing changes in my body. I felt off, my eating was funky, I started getting sick. My clothes started getting tight. I felt drained all the time. I didn't know what was going on. I talked to my mother about my symptoms, and she didn't seem so happy, even though my mother does love babies. She recommended I get a pregnancy test. I got the test. I was nervous and beyond scared. I took it. It was positive.

My father was so upset. He didn't want to see his little girl stuck being a mom at such a young age. No father would. And I was still in school. My parents wanted to see me graduate. I knew where they were coming from. I wanted the baby, but at the same time I didn't, because I also wanted to finish school. Noah wanted to be a dad so bad that he begged and begged me to keep it. Everyone in class knew about the situation because Noah told everyone that he was going to be a dad, even though I wasn't sure what I was going to do. I was stuck in between. I'd feel bad if I got rid of it, but I'd be stuck having a child so early.

A caseworker from my home school, Mrs. Morris, talked to me about pregnancy. She talked to me about finishing school, told me that I was too young to be a mother and said she was only trying to get my mind on the right track. I was all sorts of confused about what decision I wanted to make. I had the caseworker in one ear telling me to abort and think about my future, and I had Noah in the other begging me to keep the baby because he wanted nothing more than to be a family.

At one point, Mrs. Morris claimed she knew Noah and knew about his bad past. Apparently, Noah had done a terrible thing to another young girl, and he was accused of rape. I didn't believe it. I thought Mrs. Morris was making it up, which made me mad because I really thought she was just saying it to get me to abort the baby. I always told her she had the wrong Noah, but she insisted it was the right Noah.

Eventually, my final decision was to abort the baby. I told Noah, and Noah told his mother about it. Mrs. Morris set the appointment for me. The day of the appointment, Mrs. Morris picked me and my mother up. I got sick on the way there. I think it was my nerves.

When I got to Planned Parenthood, I had a lot of papers to sign. I waited in the waiting room until they called me. There were about three doctors in the room, and they got me into a gown. They gave me a pill to numb me. I laid down and they put an IV in to drug me up enough to where I couldn't feel a thing. I fell asleep and the next thing I knew, I was in a chair in the recovery room.

I was still dopey, but at that moment I realized that the abortion was already done. I felt bad and so ashamed. I hated myself for it, but I knew it was the right thing to do in that moment. I felt a little relieved too, because I didn't have to worry about not finishing school anymore, I could just graduate and not be a young mother so soon.

I sat there in the recovery room until I wasn't dizzy anymore, and then the doctors brought me in my wheelchair out to Mrs. Morris's vehicle. When I got home, I was told I had to relax. But Noah called me up and asked if I went through with the abortion. I told him I did. Noah had a sad tone in his voice after that. From that day, Noah, his mother Karen and her boyfriend Richard, all called me a baby killer. It was during this time that Noah was continuously calling me baby killer that I realized that Noah wasn't the same kind, caring guy I had once known. I also started noticing that if Noah didn't get his way, then he would act out with terrible behavior. He would eventually apologize for calling me a baby killer, but I started seeing some red flags in Noah at this point.

One of these red flags was his jealous side. He would get jealous even when a boy talked to me. He got mad at me when he saw a boy in class sit down next to me. I was in the classroom, and he was watching me from the culinary class kitchen window. I happened to look up and there was Noah, looking at me through the glass, gesturing for me to move away from the boy next to me. I didn't move, but I did ask the boy next to me to please move over because I had a jealous boyfriend. It was embarrassing, but he understood.

I didn't know what was going on with Noah; he was just acting differently. Telling me not to do certain things and to stay away from certain people. This behavior from Noah continued to worsen and worsen, to the point that he was just too controlling.

I had friends in class that were starting to notice his behavior. Multiple friends of mine told me to get away from him because it would only get worse, and that one thing could lead to another. That stuck with me, so I figured I would ask Noah why he got so jealous. Noah said he was just very protective of what's his. He made me feel like I was his property.

Since I had the abortion, it seemed he had just changed with the snap of a finger. He was like that through the rest of the year. I still wanted to be with him though, because whenever I thought about leaving him, I just got scared. I was afraid to leave because I knew that if I did, he would act out again.

Our graduating year was 2013, but Noah dropped out halfway through the school year. It was different with him not being in culinary with me. I was upset because I wanted him to graduate with me. I wanted us to walk on stage together to get our diplomas. But Noah was having problems. I didn't know exactly what was going on with him, but I think he was having mental health issues, just because he had changed into a different person so quickly. I couldn't figure out what was really going on before he just decided to drop out.

Sometimes after BOCES, I'd have the bus drop me off at the trailer park instead of going back to my home school. I basically lived with Noah on the weekends, because around this time, my parents had had to move in with my sister and Duke. They hadn't been able to find a different place to stay. Lorraine and Duke didn't have enough room for me, so I was living with my older brother Jase, who lived in Frankfort at the time. So I'd take the Frankfort bus to BOCES in the morning, then the Richfield bus in the afternoon back to Richfield school, then a teacher from Richfield would drop me back off at my brother's in Frankfort. The teacher lived in Frankfort herself, which is why she volunteered to take me home. But as I said, on weekends, I'd stay with Noah.

I was stuck in this position for a good few months until my parents finally found an apartment for themselves in Frankfort. Then everything went back to normal. I went back to living with my parents. I still went to Noah's on the weekends though. I got to know Kate and Jacob well. They did a lot for Noah; they took him in and treated him as if he were one of their own.

One night, Kate and Jacob helped Noah set up a surprise for me. Noah put together a nice dinner with candles. I couldn't figure out why he was doing this for me. We had a good conversation over dinner, and the next thing I knew, he was getting down on one knee and asking me if I'd marry him.

I started crying, said yes and got up and hugged and kissed him. The ring he put on my finger had belonged to Kate's grandma. She told Noah I could wear it until he got me a ring of my own. I called my parents to tell them the good news.

They were happy for me. Noah and I posted about it on Facebook and our friends and families congratulated us. Right there in that moment, I felt like I never had to worry about someone coming to take him away ever again. And by that, I mean other females, like having fight with Stacy over him. Even my own sister had come into play at one point. In that moment, now that I had a ring on my finger, I felt like maybe people would leave our relationship alone. In that moment, I was happy that I would be spending the rest of my life with him. I felt like nothing, and no one would take us away from each other.

Time went smoothly for a while. Then one day, culinary had a special event to prepare for, and I met a kid from the afternoon class. His name was Montana. We got talking and he asked me if I was coming back later that same day for the special event. I did come back and so did he. We hung out the whole time and exchanged numbers before I left. Montana and I talked through messages a lot after that night. Noah would look at my phone and ask who I was talking to. I told him it was a kid I met from the afternoon culinary class, and I went on to tell Noah that he was a good person. Noah said something sarcastically out of jealousy. I ignored it.

Over time, talking with Montana, my feelings started growing for him. I knew I was engaged to Noah, but Montana made me feel free. It wasn't that I didn't want to be engaged or wasn't ready to be. But Noah was still controlling, and no matter who I talked to, Noah would always say something sarcastically about the person. So, I ended up leaving Noah for Montana. Noah begged and begged for me back, calling me to ask me why I had left him for Montana. I told him that my feelings for him had faded away, and not only that, but that his controlling who I talked to and was friends with was not acceptable. By then, I had thought about it long and hard, and I decided that I didn't want to be with someone who was going to do that to me. Ring or not, I didn't want to be controlled.

A few weeks went by and part of me missed Noah. We had been through so much together. Montana could tell that something was off about me when we hung out. He would throw the question at me: "Do you still miss Noah?" I would lie and say no. He always accepted the answer, and we would just go back to whatever it was we were doing.

I was in Walmart with my parents one day when Noah messaged me, out of the blue, asking me how I was and telling me he missed me and still loved me. So, Noah, in so many words through messaging, wanted me back. He wanted things to be different this time. I thought about this as I walked through the store. I had messaged him back saying I still loved and missed him too. I messaged Montana and broke it off with him. Montana was obviously upset. I told him I was sorry. I told Noah I wanted to take things slow this time.

Noah seemed a bit different. He was living with another family in the trailer park now. There was this kid, Dean, his two sisters, two brothers and their mom. There were other people living there too. That was a lot of people living in one small trailer. When I went over the first time, I met Dean and everyone else. They were all nice. But I think living with these people changed Noah a lot. Not for better though. He seemed worse.

His controlling behavior got worse. His mouth got out of hand. He started saying some nasty stuff to me, and he started putting his hands on me whenever he had a temper. I was scared. I was often left with a bloody lip, bruises.

He locked himself with me in the bathroom one day, laid me on the bathroom floor and started having his way with me. I kept telling him to stop, but he didn't. He just continued. I cried. I was scared. After he had finished, Dean had come to the door asking what was going on and telling Noah to open. Noah didn't listen and Dean knocked the door down. I couldn't figure out why Noah had done what he did. I'm not sure if staying with this family had something to do with it, but all these people had asked of Noah was to help around the house if he was going to live there. I knew he was under pressure, being told what to do, he wasn't one for being told what to do, he never really followed the rules. and I think he got into pot through a guy who was also staying in the same trailer.

# GRADUATION PARTY, 2013

My parents planned my graduation party, which was at our apartment. My brother Allen, his girlfriend Jenny, their three-year-old Angel, my uncle Henry, my oldest brother Nelly, my parents' landlord and his wife, and Noah were all invited.

I had a blast. I drank nine or ten beers and got so wasted. I was feeling pretty good. Noah and I left the party to go upstairs to get more drinks for ourselves and everyone outside. I was heading back out the door when Noah grabbed me, spun me around and kissed me. We had sex right there in front of the door. Then we went back downstairs and outside with the drinks.

The night started rolling in and things were starting to settle down. My oldest brother had left. Everyone else was upstairs. Noah and I stayed downstairs on the couch on the porch for a while. Noah and I had sex once again. Then we went upstairs to bed.

Later the next day, Allen and Jenny were in the living room while my mom, dad and uncle were out in the kitchen. Noah and I walked into the living room and started talking with Allen and Jenny. Noah brought up something from the past and it pissed me off. If I remember correctly, it was about the girl in our class that he'd had a crush on and had left me for.

I remember getting up and walking out down the stairs to the porch. Noah followed me down, along with my brother Allen. Allen was trying to help us solve our argument. Noah sat in the chair on the porch and Allen stood in front of him.

Noah kept pissing me off. I had a pocketknife in my hand, and I went after Noah with it. I tried to slice his throat, but Allen got in the way, and I cut him instead. He was alright. Thankfully, it was only a little cut. I was so mad and drunk; I must have blacked out. It was the first time I'd ever pulled a knife on someone. I felt better, but I also felt bad. I eventually snapped out of it. I don't know if I even said sorry to Noah. it took a while before we were ok again.

A couple weeks went by, and I started to notice that everything I ate and drank wasn't sitting right with me. My stomach felt like it was burning on the inside and I constantly felt like I was going to be sick. I set up a doctor's appointment to see what was going on.

I also took a pregnancy test, and it came back positive. This was my second time being pregnant by Noah. I called Noah and there was no answer. I kept calling and calling and still, no answer. I waited until later to call again and he finally answered. I told him I was pregnant, and he didn't seem happy about it at all. He told me he wanted to focus on his future, basically said everything I had said to him the first time I found out I was pregnant, just to throw it in my face.

I started crying. I wasn't happy either, but this time I wanted to keep the baby. My parents weren't mad that I was pregnant, or that I was keeping it, which was relieving. They were the ones bringing me to my appointments because Noah and I didn't have driver's licenses.

It took a few days to a week for Noah to finally accept the pregnancy. Even though he accepted it, I knew he was angry, and I had a feeling he was going to take it out on me eventually.

One day, Noah and I went over to my brother and his girlfriend's apartment in Herkimer. My uncle was also living with them at the time. We stayed the night, and we all watched a movie called *A Cry for Help: The Tracey Thurman Story* together. It was about a housekeeper who gets involved with a guy, and over time, she gets pregnant, and he becomes very abusive toward her. No matter how many times she calls the cops to get him to stay away from her, they fail to protect her each time, to the point where he finds her, cuts her throat and stabs her multiple times in the back so that she can barely walk anymore. Surprisingly, the woman survives all this. Once she's healed enough, she sues the police department and has the guy put away for a very long time. It takes her near-death before the police finally decide to listen to Tracey.

While watching, I spoke up and said, "I don't know what I'd ever do if I was in Tracey Thurman's shoes. I'd be too scared to leave the guy because he almost killed her."

Noah responded, "Does this mean I have to start slapping you around?" He laughed then and said, "I'm just kidding." I looked at him with disgust.

One afternoon a couple weeks later, I was sitting on the porch couch, bummed, because Noah and I were having a disagreement. He was crouching in front of me, facing me. I believe we were arguing about where he was staying. I said he was acting cockier and like he cared less and less, and that staying in that trailer was changing him. I tried to get Noah to understand how I felt about the situation, but it was like it was going in one ear and out the other.

I kept coming at him about it when he suddenly slapped me across the face. He just stayed there, crouched in front of me, looking at me. I put my hand on my face, looked at Noah and said, "Why did you slap me?"

"My hand slipped."

It didn't feel like a slip to me. I knew he had done it on purpose. After Noah left, I went to the store with my uncle Henry and Allen and Jenny. On the ride there, I thought about him putting his hands on me. I was shocked he'd done it to me.

Noah called me up later that same day to apologize, and he promised to never hit me again.

In my third or fourth month of pregnancy, it was hard to tell that I was pregnant at all because my belly was still small. My doctor said it was due to a lack of food and fluids, so I needed to eat and drink more. Everything else was fine.

Noah and I ended up at my brother's place again to spend another night. We had another disagreement, so we went outside. Every time we had a disagreement about anything, we would also argue about the past, which only made the situation worse.

We were walking back and forth on Main Street, which is the street my brother's apartment is on. Main Street always has at least one or two people walking on it at night, and it's always busy during the day. Noah kept saying things to make me madder, so I started to walk faster ahead of him. He grabbed my arm and pulled me back while also reaching his other arm out to whack me in the eye so hard I started seeing dots. I moved away from him and started walking the other way, but he grabbed me again, pulled me into the alleyway and slapped me.

I said to Noah, "You promised you were never going to hit me again."

He just ignored me and continued to get in my face and yell. He slammed me up against a brick building, not caring that I was pregnant, and continued to put his hands on me.

When he finally let go, I started walking back to the apartment. He kept saying nasty stuff to me and someone walking by heard him. They got into a yelling match right there on the street. Noah then followed me through the doorway and just before I reached the stairs, I told Noah I was done with him. He didn't like that. He punched me in the stomach, and I went down on the steps. My brother was just coming around the corner and caught sight of Noah doing this. He ran down the stairs, got in Noah's face and kicked him out. I was laying there crying. My brother helped me up the stairs into his apartment. When I got inside, I went to the bathroom and that's when I noticed I had started leaking blood from down there the next day, I called the doctor's office, told them what was going on and set up an appointment.

The day of my appointment, my mother came in the room with me. The doctor did an exam and told me that I didn't have enough fluids in me and that I'd eventually lose the baby. I told her I hadn't started leaking until my boyfriend punched me. This doctor told me again that the leaking wasn't because he punched me, but because I didn't have enough fluids. It was like she wasn't taking the time to hear what I was saying. I hadn't leaked before Noah hit me. I would have had fluids in me if Noah hadn't hit me in the stomach. I tried telling the doctor this, but she was stuck on the fluids. I knew she was wrong. I had nothing wrong going on until Noah hit me.

The doctor sent me downstairs to get blood work. When I got there, I went to use the ladies' room. Blood gushed out of me, all over the bathroom floor. I started yelling for my mother, my mother came rushing in and started freaking out, so she yelled for a nurse. A nurse came rushing in, cleaned up the blood and took me to the emergency room. I told the doctor in the emergency room that I had just come from my appointment and told her that the doctor upstairs had done an exam on me. The doctor in the emergency room told me that she shouldn't have done an exam on me while I was pregnant. I had no idea that she shouldn't have. I never saw the doctor who did that exam on me ever again.

A couple weeks later, on October 29, 2013, I lost the baby in the early morning. The night before, I'd had non-stop labor pains. I could barely walk or sleep, no matter what I did. I just couldn't get comfortable. I cried all night. My mother gave me Tylenol to help with the pain, but nothing I did worked. Eventually, when it was very late, I was able to close my eyes, but it wasn't long until I woke up again. I noticed that the pain was no longer there, and I could move. I got up to go to the bathroom, and I noticed that something was blocking me from peeing. I pushed hard and something came out. I slowly looked down, and it was the baby. I yelled for my mother and started freaking out. My mother came in and saw that I was in shock. She ran and grabbed the scissors. I cut my own cord that sad, early morning.

I was rushed to the hospital. The guy in the ambulance told me he was sorry for my loss and gave me a stuffed bear to hold. I was at the hospital all day and night. My parents called my brother Allen and told him I had lost the baby. I believe my brother ended up getting a hold of Noah to tell him and to have words with him about what he had done to me.

Noah got his foot back in the door with my brother after that. I think it was because my brother felt bad for Noah about the baby, and so he welcomed him back. At the same time though, my brother and my parents still wanted to hurt him for what he had done to me, but I told them not to. It was what it was, as wrong as it was for me to say, but I didn't want to go through anymore then what I already had. I was too tired and drained and emotionally damaged. I had no fight left in me.

After finally leaving the hospital, my parents took me over to my brother's because Noah was there, and my brother wanted to see me too. When I saw Noah, I was disgusted with him because none of this would have happened if he hadn't hit me. I secretly, deep down, hated him for what he had done. Part of me couldn't even look at Noah.

I shut a lot of people out at this point in my life. Friends, family. I lost myself. Losing the baby changed me. I was so alone and in such a dark place. I didn't even want to live. My feelings were changing too. I looked at my life differently. I still stayed with Noah even though I didn't want to. I should have left him for what he did. But I didn't. I was scared. I didn't have the guts to walk away, but I felt guilty for still being with him. I felt disgusted with myself for staying with him. But I just didn't want to fight anymore, I was beyond done. I stayed just to go along with life. I was at the point where I didn't care what happened to me. Something within me had just given up.

About a month later, I was at my brother's again with Noah. I had grabbed Noah's phone and headphones to listen to music in another room while he was out in the living room playing a game with Allen. Out of curiosity, I went through Noah's Facebook messages. I found old messages that showed that he had cheated on me months ago with an old friend of mine while we were in a disagreement. I freaked out. I cried and cried and when I went out to ask him why he had cheated, he said it was because we'd had a disagreement and the other girl had and wanted to make me jealous.

That right there had done it. That was what made me pull right back from Noah. I cried for months and months over it. I was such a damn wreck. Losing the baby and then finding out about that, everything was just falling apart around me. I felt more and more lost. I kept asking myself why I stayed with Noah. I was getting more disgusted with him as time went on. I had nothing but built-up anger and a burning feeling inside when I thought of him.

From what I can remember, every fight we had after this point was always about the past and him cheating, or he would accuse me of wanting to be with one of my guy friends and he'd call me names like slut, whore or ugly bitch. He'd say things like, "Who would want you? You're ugly." Anything to put my self-esteem down. He would always accuse me of things like sleeping around on him with his friends, but whenever he threw that in my face, I'd tell him that I wasn't the one who cheated, he was. He always took his anger out on me because he knew I was right, and he didn't like being told he was in the wrong. So, there were times he'd choke me, kick me in the stomach, spit in my face, or headbutt me in the eye.

I used to lie to my parents about my injuries and say I hit my eye by opening the door too fast, but they didn't buy it. For the couple of times, they knew about Noah hitting me, my father put his hands on him. Noah even promised my dad he would never hit me again. But still, every time Noah and I got into an argument, he would drag me across the floor by my hair and step on my throat. He had smashed my head on a toilet seat and even threatened to smash my head on a pipe that was sticking up from the ground. But only whenever my parents weren't around.

Noah had taken a plastic CD case one time, cracked it and held the broken shard up to my throat. He said, "How does it feel?" as he slowly started to slice my throat with it. He stopped, but I was shaken up. He had threatened to kill me and my family plenty of times.

Every time I tried to leave Noah; he would hit me into staying with him. He would tell me things like, "I'm glad that piece of shit baby died in your stomach." He would joke about sleeping with my sister. He would do anything to be in control of a situation. He said to me that if he couldn't have me then no one would. I was scared to leave. I felt like there was no way out. He promised so many times that he would stop hitting me, but he never did. Every time I threatened to tell my dad what was going on, Noah would just hit me more.

I should have listened to those who told me so long ago to leave before it got worse. Now I just felt trapped. There were times when I begged Noah to kill me after the beatings, he gave me. I wish I could have just gotten up and walked away, but it wasn't easy. Part of me still loved him, even though he wasn't showing me the same kind of love. Part of me wanted to leave and part of me wanted to stay and hope he would change. I always put the love that I had for him before anything else, even knowing that what he was doing to me was wrong. I wanted him to change and all I could do was hope for it, even when my body was weak.

All I wanted was no more lies, no more cheating, no more hitting. I told him this numerous times. Noah promised repeatedly that he would stop hitting me. I didn't believe him, but I wanted to. He had his ways of winning me over and making me fall for him again and again and again. Finally, this one time, he promised to get the help he needed. He said he would do whatever it took to make it work, no more past stuff, no more lies, no more cheating. He stopped hitting me. He lived up to his word. And so, I fell for him once again and eventually ended up pregnant.

I told my parents I was pregnant. They weren't mad. They were in the middle of moving again, back to Richfield, and this time my brother Allen and his family, our uncle, my mom and dad and I were all moving in together. I begged my dad to let Noah stay with us. He was a strong no at first, but after thinking about it for a while, he changed his mind. But the deal was, no arguing, no hands on me and Noah had to get a job to support me and the baby. Noah agreed, and he did good for a while.

I believe I was in my sixth month of pregnancy when Noah started acting up again. I started seeing behavioral red flags again. I thought to myself, *please don't let this be happening again*. Noah never did get the help he promised he would get. Sometimes, when I talked to Noah now, he would have an attitude and be sarcastic toward me for no reason at all. Everything he had promised my dad and everything I thought he had meant this time had gone right back out the window.

One day, Noah and I were upstairs while my family was downstairs watching TV. Noah was arguing with me about something, but he kept quiet enough that my family couldn't hear from downstairs. He then locked me in the bedroom and wouldn't let me out to eat. I kept telling him I was hungry and so was the baby, but he didn't care. He wanted to keep me locked in until he was ready to let me out. I didn't want to scream because I didn't want to take the chance that he might hurt this baby. I was really trying to be healthy with this pregnancy, so I was watching my step with Noah. I'd do anything to avoid him hurting this child.

The next morning when I woke up, Noah put his hands on me sexually. I didn't want to do anything, so I told him to stop. He tied my hands to the bed and had his way with me. I wanted to scream, but again I didn't because I was afraid that if I did, I would be putting the baby's life in jeopardy. He had threatened to hurt the baby and me just to get his way before. During an argument we had, he'd said, "I'll push down on your stomach and kill this worthless baby like the other one. This baby doesn't deserve to live." Noah threatened me by threatening my family too. He never cared about anything or anyone but himself, and he was always cocky about it too. He was like this throughout the rest of my pregnancy.

# NOVEMBER 17, 2014

Our little girl, Natasha Hope Duncan, was born. Noah was a bit teary-eyed; my family came to visit and my sister and Duke did as well. I had a C-section. So much pain, but I was so happy to see my daughter here and healthy. I cried when I first held her. I had emotions running through me like crazy. This child changed my whole world around completely. My mother nicknamed her "Fighter," because she had basically fought through everything I had. In those first moments I knew that I had to protect my baby from her father. I had to make sure that he and nothing else would ever hurt her.

Noah and I stayed at the hospital for a week. When we got home, our bedroom had been moved downstairs because it was warmer. My mother helped Noah and me with Natasha the first night. I was still in so much pain—I still needed more rest time to heal—and it was also Noah's first-time taking care of a baby.

The second night, Noah was giving me a hard time about getting up with the baby like he said he would. I was still in lots of pain. We were arguing at four in the morning. My parents' upstairs could hear us, so they came down to see what was going on. My father told Noah that he needed to help because I was still in so much pain and my body wasn't fully healed yet. My father also told him, "You play you pay," and that this baby was his responsibility just as much as mine.

I couldn't carry Natasha if I tried at this point. Noah didn't care about helping me though. He cared about his sleep more than anything, and it really pissed him off that he had to get up and help. And that pissed me right off because he was being selfish and did nothing but think of himself. We argued all the time about who would get up with the baby.

I asked him one morning to help and he threw a fit. I got up, grabbed the baby and went into a different room. Noah followed behind me, grabbed the back of my neck and demanded me to hand over the baby. He took her and went back to our room, sat on the bed and rocked her so fast because he was still pissed off about having to help. I yelled at him for rocking her too hard. He didn't give a fuck though. He was just being selfish.

I gave up asking for his help after that. I shouldn't have even had to ask. He should have been willing, but he never was. I decided to do it myself. But I got sick of it one day and started flipping out. My dad stepped in and told Noah that the best thing would be for him to go stay at his ex-stepdad's. So, Noah's ex stepdad Daniel came and picked Noah up later that day. Noah ended up staying at Daniels for good.

After Noah left, Lorraine and Duke came over. Not even an hour went by before my sister started accusing me of hooking up with Duke while the baby was in another room. She and Duke still weren't getting along. I told my sister that she had never accused me of Duke until she started sneaking Noah into her place had happened. She must have felt guilty about something. I also told her that Noah had joked about sleeping with her. Obviously, something had happened. Duke then brought up that he'd found a shirt that wasn't his on their bedroom floor. I asked Duke, "Did it say, 'Get a tattoo you fucking pussy' on it?" Duke said yeah, and I told Duke then that its Noah's because I'd seen Noah wear that shirt. At this point, my sister got in my face, still accusing me of Duke, and I got back in hers. We ended up having a fistfight.

Since my parents were moving to a different home in Richfield, my brother Allen and his family, and my uncle Henry, took over their place. I stayed with my brother for about two weeks until I moved in with my parents. I had to let Noah and his stepdad Daniel know where I was living because we had worked out a schedule: Noah would take the baby for a week, then I'd get her for a week.

There were times when Daniel would come pick me and the baby up to go visit Noah. I thought some time away from Noah would help us get back on track, but no, he started arguments with me at his stepdad's place too. We had even gotten into fistfights there because of arguments Noah had started. Of course, this all happened when Daniel wasn't around. Noah and I would be fighting on the floor, and he'd punch me in the stomach. Noah had even taken a coffee pot, glass and all, and thrown it at me. That time, I started crying. Afterward, I waited for Daniel to get back from the store and told him what had happened. Daniel asked me why Noah had thrown the pot, so I told him that Noah was starting his crap again. Daniel then turned to me, looked at me with a serious look and said these exact words: "I see nothing, I heard nothing," before smirking at me. I stood there looking at Daniel like, *you have to be kidding me, you too.* I thought to myself, *He's no different from Noah.* I eventually stopped going to Daniel's house and stuck to the schedule. Noah had Natasha for one week and then I had her for one week. It gave Noah and I some time to be apart for a while. That's what we needed.

Noah and I worked out our issues like we always had. My parents found a place in Richfield. Noah ended up getting kicked out of his ex-stepdads for whatever reason and stayed with us again. My parents were getting sick of him living with us, but I pleaded with them to take him back in, thinking it would be a fresh start for us.

But it would always only last for so long before Noah would start up his lying again and telling me what to wear, who to hang out with and who to be friends with. It was one thing after another. He started hiding things from me, going on all these online sites to cheat on me whenever I fell asleep.

One night, I caught him at it, and I flipped out. He promised he wouldn't do it again, but I knew that these same old bad habits just weren't going to change. Nothing ever stopped him. He continued to use these sites. And that wasn't the only issue I was having with him. He also wouldn't do anything with

Natasha unless he "felt like it." I was overwhelmed and I knew I was close to snapping. It was only a matter of time.

I was getting downright sick of the way Noah was acting. Days would go by, and I'd just be on edge with him. He only made things worse by continuing to run his mouth at me and by being controlling. I was sick of it.

I was in the bedroom one day and he was in my face, running his mouth. So, I was arguing back. Next thing I knew, he got brave and poked his finger on my forehead. I just snapped. Everything happened so fast. I speared him onto the bed, crawled on top of him and started pounding the shit out of his face. I was yelling at him. I had him pinned down. I wrapped my hands around his throat and started squeezing for dear life. My father came rushing in, along with my aunt, who happened to be there that day. They both started trying to pull me off Noah, but my hands were wrapped around his throat so tightly that he was turning purple. His face was all bruised up. I almost killed him. But my father finally got my hands loose. Noah and I were on a rocky boat after that. We'd talk to each other, but it was never the same.

About two weeks after, Noah was outside on the swing with Natasha. I was inside doing dishes. As I washed them, I had all these thoughts running through my head. *I should just leave. Think of yourself and your daughter and forget about him. You don't deserve to live like this. He's never going to change his ways.*

Once I finished the dishes, I went outside and told Noah to get out. He tried to fight with me, but I wouldn't fight back. I had no time or energy to put up with any more of his nonsense. So,

Noah left and managed to get his mother and her boyfriend Richard to let him stay with them.

Noah and I stayed on and off for a while. He lived with his mother until Natasha was three years old. Noah and I obviously still talked because of Natasha, even though Noah's mother and her boyfriend wanted Noah to have nothing to do with me. They didn't even want Noah talking to me. So, Noah would sneak phone calls, and he even snuck over to see us sometimes.

After a while, I got tired of sneaking around. I told Noah he should tell his mother and Richard that he was still seeing me, because it was getting more difficult to see him. Noah kept telling me that he was going to tell them, and after while he said he had told them.

We had been sneaking around for a couple of months when I found out I was pregnant again. I called my father up from the doctor's office crying, but I told him that I wasn't going to keep it. I called Noah up right after, but Richard answered instead of Noah. I asked for Noah and when he picked up, he acted like he hadn't talked to me in months so that he would look good in front of his mother and Richard. So now Richard and Karen were wondering why I was calling if Noah hadn't been talking to me.

I told Noah I was pregnant. Richard and Karen overheard, and they were not happy at all. Noah asked if it was his. I told him that I wasn't with anyone else but him. I knew right there and then that he'd never told his mom and Richard about still seeing me. I told Noah I wasn't keeping the baby.

When I got home from the doctor's, I did nothing but cry my eyes out.

The next morning, I called and set up an appointment with Planned Parenthood to abort the baby. I wasn't ready for another child. Mine and Noah's relationship was and always had been on and off. We weren't stable enough; our relationship was toxic, and I wasn't going to go through raising a second baby alone.

Noah called me later and asked if the baby was really his. I told him the same thing I did the last time we spoke. I had about a week until it was time to abort the baby. Noah asked if I was really going to go through with the abortion. I told him I was.

Noah called me on the day of the abortion and asked how I was feeling. For once he was there for me. He even called me up and talked to me several days after the abortion had happened. But then, on another day, he called again and had an attitude, once again doubting that the baby was even his. He said he was upset that I had gotten rid of the baby, and he started calling me a baby killer and saying that everything bad that had happened to us was my fault. I started yelling a bunch of things back at him through the phone.

My parents heard me yelling from the other room, and they knew instantly that Noah was starting his crap again. Noah continued saying hurtful things to me, getting me, all worked up and pissed off before hanging up on me. I came storming out of my bedroom and flipped out. The police came and took me to Bassett Hospital's psychiatric ward.

# HOSPITAL REPORT

atient had an elective abortion several days ago. Had an argument with her significant other as he was upset about her decision to terminate pregnancy. She pulled a knife and threatened to hurt herself. Reported she did not have intentions of self-harm but was frustrated.

Initial impression was that of adjustment reaction in setting of abortion and abusive relationship. Joanie quickly compensated and recognized how damaging her current relationship is. She created a plan to seek full custody of her child and leave her relationship. She related to VIP for domestic violence victims. Her suicidal thoughts resolved on admission and remained absent. She was forward-thinking about her daughter and expressed support in her parents. Hydroxyzine helped with sleep. She was referred to health home navigator.

After getting home from the hospital, my mind was set on taking Noah to court, and I did just that. We ended up with joint custody. He had to pay child support, but he hardly ever did. He barely ever came to take Natasha on the days he was supposed to have her. He would lie and make up excuses to not come get her sometimes. We ended up back in court because of this, only to have the same outcome, which made me mad because I wanted some time to myself too.

One time when Noah came to get Natasha, we had already started arguing before he arrived. Karen gave him rides to pick up Natasha, and whenever they came, they parked next door, so I had to carry Natasha and everything of hers over there. Noah was lazy and did not help carry anything. I was already frustrated with him as it was.

I opened Karen's passenger door and got in Noah's face about him always being late and always lying to me about where he was. Noah's mother spoke up, so then I got into it with her. She pissed me off so much that I opened the back door, crawled in and started swinging at her in the driver's seat. Noah blocked all my hits, so I spat at her, got out of the car and threw a rock at her vehicle. Karen then said the cops were on their way. I did not care. The only thing I cared about was getting my hands on her. Luckily, my brother-in-law, Scooter, was there to pull me away from the vehicle. After that day, Noah's mother stopped coming to pick up Natasha. Instead, it was Richard's daughter who came with Noah a couple times. But eventually, that all stopped.

I finally said enough is enough. I'd had enough of Noah, and I finally stuck to my word. He was no longer welcome in my life or Natasha's life, and from then on, he disappeared from them completely.

Noah really put me through a lot. All the drama he caused me and my family. All the lies and the manipulation to get his way. The cheating and abuse he put me through. The things he told my friends about me, like calling me a slut and a whore and telling them that I slept around. He told one of his friends about how he would hit me. He always tried to make me look bad whenever he wanted to impress someone else. I eventually found out that he had cheated on me with Kate's daughter Ruby behind my back while we were dating. I knew something was up with her from the first time I met her. The comments she made toward me, and about Noah and her, I just had a gut feeling that something wasn't right. And she wasn't the only one in the trailer park that Noah cheated on me with.

Noah has done so many sneaky, painful things behind my back. I'm glad I got away from it all. As far as Karen and Richard are concerned, they finally figured out what Noah was all about, and we are on good terms now. Karen currently sees Natasha occasionally.

Natasha is now eight years old and doing well in school. As for me, I have found my true love. His name is tom, and he is very good with Natasha and me. We are cared for and loved very much. Everything is the way it should be. Tom takes care of us. He helps with Natasha and I'm thankful for that. Nothing feels better than to finally have the family I've always dreamed of having.

But I do feel, after all these years, that Noah left a part of himself within me. I say that because all the trauma Noah put me through over the years created a reflection of him in me. I notice that whenever Tom and I have a disagreement,

I act in the same way that Noah did with me. I don't do the controlling part, but I accuse Tom in the same way that Noah used to accuse me. This has been an ongoing issue for a while. My mind gets so deep into believing that Tom is doing things when he's not. My mind keeps reliving the past.

I'm currently on medication to help cope with the past trauma and my outbursts. I'm also talking with a counselor. As far as Tom and I, we have been taking our time. He understands everything I've been through and he's very patient with me. Tom helps me get through so much and I'm thankful for him. I know that being with Tom, Natasha and I are safe and we won't ever have to worry about living a terrifying life with Noah again.

Printed in the USA
CPSIA information can be obtained
at www.ICGtesting.com
LVHW070933271023
761899LV00070B/1145/J